# Loving Leah

# Loving Leah

Poems by

Neil Creighton

Cover design by Shay Culligan

ISBN: 978-1-950462-89-6

Kelsay Books Inc.

kelsaybooks.com

502 S 1040 E, A119
American Fork,Utah 84003

In memory of my mother, Brenda Lynette Creighton,
1919-2014
and for my sister, Jean Schad,
my brother, Duncan Creighton,
and for our children,
Jen, Peter, Dan, Catherine, Ben, Tim, Brad, Troy and Georg.

# Acknowledgments

*Prosopisia:* "In the Nursing Home"

*Verse-Virtual:* "Mother," "After the Storm"

*Peacock Journal:* "Leah"

*Better than Starbucks:* "Turned and Gone Away"

*Anti-Heroin Chic:* "Ruins", "Lost, Without Compass or Star," "Tapestry"

*Rat's Ass Review:* "Labyrinth"

*Autumn Sky Daily:* "Grief " (first published as "Hope")

*One Sentence Poetry:* "See"

# Contents

*You must bear with me.*
*Pray you now, forget and forgive: I am old and foolish.*

—King Lear, Act IV, Sc vii, ll 84

# Part 1. Five Visions of Leah

# Last Days

It is dangerous to leave Leah on her own.
She sets the microwave timer for three hours.
It bursts into flames.
She loses her balance and falls, breaking her hip.
Cordelia's sisters telephone her.
Can she spend one day a week with Leah?
Cordelia loves Leah and happily complies,
although she remembers all those years
where her sisters made her feel unwelcome
in what had once been their family home.

In springtime she pushes Leah in her wheelchair.
The days sparkle with blossom and bird song.
She wants Leah to again see beauty.
Leah is terrified that Cordelia will let her go
and set her careering downhill.
Most weeks she takes Leah out to lunch
but Leah's world is so shrunken
that she is happiest in her familiar chair
in the familiar room with the television
on an endlessly repetitive loop.
Occasionally she says strange things.
One day, out of the blue, she says
*I hate Wills. I really hate Wills.*
Cordelia notices how Leah,
once generous and kind in spirit,
now apes the more critical thinking
of her other two daughters
but at the end of each day, she looks at Cordelia
with her gentle, kind eyes
and summons a little of her old charm.
*Thank you,* she says. *You've saved my life.*

Leah has another stroke and is in a nursing home.
Sometimes she forgets who Cordelia is.
*This is my sister,* she says, smiling proudly.
On parting there is always the same, anxious response.
*You're not leaving? So soon?*
Once, troubled, she looks at Cordelia and says
*Whatever will people think of me?*
Then she turns and stares at the wall.
One day Cordelia arrives when a nurse is bathing Leah.
*Leave me alone;* she cries in anguish.
*I don't want a bath. It's my bloody body.*
Cordelia is shocked.
She has never heard Leah swear.
Leah was always so calm and controlled.
*Your sisters insist,* the nurse says.

Cordelia visits for the last time.
Leah is unconscious, her face shrunken,
her cheeks deeply hollow.
She is a tiny, fragile, skeletal thing.
A ghastly look of death is gripping her
but Leah will still not let go.
Something inside her is refusing to surrender.
Cordelia weeps a torrent of tears.
She gently places her hand on Leah's old hand.
Her heart is filled with love and grief.
*Oh mother,* she says, *mother, mother, mother,*
*my dear mother, oh my mother.*

# Surrender

It is easy for Leah to welcome back
her two disappointed daughters.
She craves company and close connection.
Living alone has been difficult.

It is easy for her to imagine
that she can love them into happiness.
She has the empath's weakness.
She believes that she can fix things.

If, over time, tyranny emerges,
like bullying or sulking in bedrooms,
it is easy for her to shrug it off.
It only means that she is important to them.

It is easy for her to surrender.
It is her nature and it happens so gradually,
a concession here and there until one day
there is no longer any space for Cordelia.

It is easy to hope for Cordelia's understanding.
She has grown old and dependent
and as usefulness diminishes,
she lives in fear of abandonment.

It is easy for her to keep secrets.
Secrets are something over which she,
who has surrendered everything else,
still has some power and control.

It becomes easy to pretend that all is well.
It becomes easy to justify the unjustifiable.
It becomes easy to expect assent.
Such things are as easy as lying.

It is not easy, though, to wake in fright.
Too often, there is a child in her bedroom.
*Cordelia, is that you? I'm so sorry.*
*Please understand that I had no choice.*

Nor will discovery be easy for Cordelia.
For long nights she will stare into the darkness
in a difficult search for that terrifying place
where her loved mother came to dwell.

# Free

Leah's disposition is calm and controlled,
her heart loving and loyal,
even for her husband,
a complex and challenging man
capable of joy, generosity and love
but also irascible, difficult and jealous
and sometimes domestic tyrant.
A war veteran, his final fifteen years
are filled with a perplexing mixture
of love, sickness and rage.
If she sometimes bends under the dual strains
of husband and family,
she will never abandon him.
At the moment of his death
there is tender acknowledgment:
she gently places her forehead on his,
mind to mind, body to body.
Then she stands and quietly leaves.

It is the beginning of a new life.
Tightly bound chains fall.
She travels overseas for the first time.
She rediscovers long suppressed,
once barely permitted creativity.
She paints, exhibits, sells.
She has a group of artist friends.
She visits Cordelia.
The towering gum trees,
her grandson walking to school
down a tree-lined dusty track,
the view across the deep, narrow valley
to ever-changing, light and shadow-filled
Mumbulla Mountain
fill her with joy and creativity.

*Why don't you live with us?*

*Thanks, Cordelia, but no.*
*I have a very good relationship with you.*
*I wouldn't want to do anything to spoil it.*

At home, in the evenings,
if sometimes she feels a little lonely
or, because her heart is so loving,
she misses that deep bond of intimate connection,
she has no intention of taking another lover.
One man has been more than enough.
Then, after some years, her youngest returns,
needy, damaged, possessive, jealous.
She opens her door but it closes
to a faint chink of chain and click of lock.
Bit by bit the possessiveness increases
and aging Leah with the loving heart
and the need to be needed
will surrender to the kind of relationship
with which she was once so familiar.

Cordelia, increasingly excluded,
discovers, on her mother's passing,
the totality of her exclusion.
She will grieve, not for the exclusion
but for Leah herself, for her weakness,
for her helpless deceit and folly,
for her lies and guilt and the contrast
between her last days and her prime.

One day she will come to understand
her mother's oft-repeated words
about her youngest daughter,
viewing them as a kind of powerless warning,
an explanation when she was no longer capable
of stating the full horror of explicit truth.

*Your sister is very like your father.*

# The Centre of the Universe

Cordelia's young life barely knows sorrow.
She wanders the lake's uninhabited shore.
She explores the bush.
She observes birds.
She finds a shortcut through the reedy swamp
to the little two teacher school.
She tracks brumbies on the hill above the school.
She is young, exultant and free.

Leah is at the core of her happiness.
Leah gives her freedom.
Leah is always there.
Leah is a fragrant balm.
Cordelia loves Leah without thought.
Cordelia's trust is absolute.
Leah is the center of her universe.

Cornelia's teenage years are more troubled.
Her father becomes sick.
His mood changes suddenly, erratically.
He cannot stand opinion other than his own.
His temper rages can last for days.
If he drinks the family is on tenterhooks.
His coughing and struggle for breath
fill the house with dread.
It is a relief when he is hospitalized,
sometimes for weeks at a time.

Leah holds her family together.
She is the rock on which they stand.
She treats all her children equally.
In times of stress, she makes jokes.
She is never judgmental.
Cordelia admires her, loves her,
wants to be like her.
Leah is the stable center of her universe.

# Nurture

Somewhere, way beyond memory,
in the subliminal world of infancy,
when baby Cordelia cries
Leah lifts her to the breast
where Cordelia suckles
then sleeps in snug contentment,
surrounded by the glory of Leah's scent.

Part 2. Letting Leah Go

# In the Nursing Home

That great gift-giver, time,
has brought her to a point
where she shuffles slowly in her frame
or sits quietly in her chair
sustained by remnants of memory,
waiting for she knows not what.
Weep for her, shed your tears,
but in this life of vulnerable mortality
time has gifted her an abundance of years.
The weight of time's gifts has bent her,
carried her at last to the great, dark portal
through which all life must flow,
carried her ceaselessly along
with one final gift to bestow,
the release into serenity,
into quiet, conscious-less eternity,
time's final gift of letting her go.

# Mother

I watch the rise and fall of her chest,
listen intently for her breath,
part fearful, part hopeful,
waiting for death to come,
knowing that life can be lived for far too long.
Where is she now?
With her much-loved mother?
Smelling the rich warmth of the milking shed?
Seeing her brothers walking across the near paddock?
Let her be anywhere but this
diminished and difficult present
where vitality is gone and each day
she seems to fade a little more.

She wakes.
There is a smile as if sweetness
cannot be washed away, no,
not even by the relentless grip
that sweeps her inexorably along.
Suddenly, seeing that smile,
I think of what she was,
how she walked through this world
in quiet anonymity, a creative spirit,
deeply gentle, calm and self-controlled,
flexible, open and inquisitive,
her heart tempered in love,

and bending to kiss her,
perhaps for the final time,
walking away from her,
past the repetitive muttering
of the vacant ghosts in their wheelchairs,
this sad, last abiding place,

my heart is strangely swelling
with a sense of privilege and gift,
sad that life can come to this
but proud and elated to have known her,
been nurtured and loved by her,
marveling that my anonymous life
can be so rich, so full of blessing,
so beautifully filled in its entirety
with the wonderful love of women,
and raising my eyes heavenwards
in silent, sad, complex thankfulness
I ask that I can carry her gentleness with me,
passing it on to those that I love,
setting free her unknown greatness
to ripple and wash through and over
the countless generations yet to come.

# Cordelia's Grief

*Here I disclaim all my paternal care.*
                    —King Lear

I close my eyes.
You are at my window again.
What do you want from me?
Forgiveness? That I wash away your guilt?

Your secrecy betrayed my love for you.
You went away, forever,
leaving me nothing but dark revelations
of your partiality and my exclusion.

I thought we shared the bond of love.
Had I become of no worth to you?
You banished me from inheritance,
cruelly, without word of warning.

Do you think I cared for your trinkets,
those bits of clay and patches of green?
I loved you, thought you great of heart,
believed that you were kind, fair, upright.

Why didn't you tell me? What kept you quiet?
Had age swept away all your empathy?
Had frailty rendered you powerless?
Was my love not deserving of truth?

I want you to go away.
I want this nightly grief to leave.
You hurt me, deeply.
I want to be free of you

but every night, in my essence,
that place where my sprit dwells,
heavy chains of blood and love
bind me to the full sad weight of you.

# Leah

I think of you, Leah,
your young self standing
against tempests in calm control,
your artist eye filled with dreams
of children in golden forests,
sun dance of poppies,
moon floating high
into the velvet night,
foam ripple of waves
washing white sand.

I think of you, Leah,
leaf-fragile, partial, secretive,
how you inch in your walker,
flop in front of the screen's
mind-numbing monotony,
dream of painting again,
linger over photographs,
shuffle the years
and that deceiver, memory,
into forms that make you happy.

Leah, is it comfort
that the gathering tide
flowed over you, swept you
out into the deep calm
where the great swells gather,

far beyond the tears of the living
trapped in this tumult,
this ebb and flow of waves
that pound upon the sand
and suck back relentlessly
into the ceaseless sea?

# Ruins

Here lie the ruins of Leah's house,
windows broken, tiles askew,
now just a crumbling wall or two.

She built it when she was young
from distillations of her love
and she filled it with her song.

Sad that she grew old and frail.
Sad her judgment fled.
Sad she gave her keys away.

Sad the music changed.
Sad the windows broke.
Sad the roof tiles slipped and cracked.

Sad the wind and rain,
sweeping through the house,
blew all the notes away.

If in dreams I listen closely
on the wind I still hear
fragments of her song.

Then I grieve for her
and for every brick of her house.
All that music gone to waste.

# Soundly Sleeping

Who placed the arrow in the groove?
Who set the trigger waiting?
Did my sisters build that crossbow?
Did that spoil your sleeping?

The arrow flew straight, went deep,
left gaping wounds still seeping
in one you professed to love.
Did that disturb your sleeping?

Many nights I searched for you
to find what you were thinking
but your door is locked and barred.
You are soundly sleeping.

I held you in high esteem
yet you left me deeply grieving.
How could you cut me from your family?
Did secrecy ruin your sleeping?

I had great depth of love for you
but I want to finish with weeping.
I'm sad that you grew so diminished.
I'm sad that you are sleeping.

# Pyrrhic Victory

Weep for the family,
for its broken walls,
its scattered people.

Weep for the vanquished
groaning in sackcloth
outside the rubble walls.

Weep for the victors
holding aloft the key
while the city burns.

# Turned and Gone Away

Leah, your house, gripped by flood,
floats from its foundations, sinking ever lower.
I cry out to you, swim, throw a rope, beg you to leave
but you can only wring your hands,
turn and float away.

Leah, small and diminished,
you tremble before a precipice filled with darkness.
I cry out that I understand your fears of age,
diminished powers, loneliness,
the horror that shuffling dependency
may lead you into actions once unspeakable
but you can only wring your hands,
turn and step away.

Leah, in deep denial you reel from the mirror, truth.
You close your eyes and cover your ears.
I cry out that I understand
how time and circumstance have trapped you,
that you have grown far too old for truth,
that you need to pretend you still are
that once wonderful person
but you can only wring your hands,
stagger and flee away.

Mother, you shuffle down a long corridor
in the slow and painful way of your last years.
I cry out that I understand how extreme age
forced you into secrets, deceptions,
and, much worse, betrayal of some you once loved.
I shout I love you and forgive you
but the words echo and bounce down the empty corridor.
You have ceased wringing your hands.
You have turned and gone away.

# Lost, Without Compass or Star

I put my hand to the tiller,
turn this creaking vessel
into a darkly rumbling surge
of grief, bewilderment and betrayal,
finding in love and forgiveness
wind sufficient to fill my little sail
and lift me up and over the tumult
into water deep and gentle
and sorrowfully compassionate.

Clouds dissipate. The stars are out.
The surge flows smoothly.
My arm, steady on the tiller,
holds the course firm and true.
I know extreme age stole
all her best qualities,
her vision, judgment, empathy
and, most especially, honesty.
Without vigor to guide her way,
she drifted vulnerably across the dark.

There are no quiet, protected waters,
only sailing on a sea
that alternately shimmers or looms.
One day, inevitably, the gift
of an overflowing surge will come.
Best if it arrives before capacity
to raise your own sail is lost.
She was always gentle and kind.
What cast her loose, set her drifting
on a last dark voyage
that belied all her previous voyaging?

# Labyrinth

I linger no longer
in this labyrinth.
Darkness suffocates.
The sulphurous air
stinks of bitterness.
Besides, your locked door
has no key.

I wade the dark river,
my pack heavy.
I shed weights,
slip on rocks,
halt before the last sheer face.

High above, light pools,
casts dappled patterns,
slants in descending columns
through cloud and tree.
Birds arc and flit in the silken air,
the dome gloriously blue,
the night diamond flecked.

I drop my pack.
The leaden thump
echoes through the darkness.
I look upwards, breathe,
place one hand
on the smooth surface
and climb.
The living wait.
With each inching ascent
I feel other hands
reaching down.

# After the Storm

Two paths forked
on the mountainside.
Shivering and wet,
I sheltered under an overhang.

The storm was abating.
Blue-black clouds
rushed in rumble and flash
further down the valley.

Columns of light
like celestial spokes
descended and dissolved
above the far mountainside.

Behind, the sinuous past
spooled through swamp,
rock-pool, canyon,
river-wandering valley,

boulder-strewn roads,
litter of bright flowers,
sun-dappled ridges,
and this last fierce storm.

*I can choose the path*
*but not the mixture*
*of burden or beauty hidden*
*behind each bend or rise.*

*Is my only real choice*
*in response, in how I walk,*
*in what weights I carry,*
*in what weights I discard?*

*Do the weights I carry,*
*those known and unknown,*
*direct and predetermine*
*both path and how I walk?*

I sat for a long while.
The sky had cleared.
Last light pooled in puddles
and gleamed on wet rock.

The dark mountain loomed.
I stood and walked.
The Evening Star glowed
in the growing gloom.

# Grief

Grief, like a hidden undertow,
sucks out beyond the blue swell
uncurling noisily upon the sand,
out beyond the raucous sea birds
circling, soaring and dipping
above the white-topped crests,
out into a dark, trackless waste
where the moving water mountain
towers glass smooth and sheer
and over its vast plateau top
waves foam and rumble
in irresistible chaos.
Then only surrender remains,
letting the mighty surge
sweep where it will,
holding in a few tiny cells
the knowledge of a gentler swell
washing slowly back
into some sheltered cove
where the patterned ripples
kiss the yellow sand,
acceptance fills the clear blue sky
and the whole glorious world
shines again bright and new.

# See

I have learnt
that even on a rainy day
the honeysuckle
dresses in cream and gold

I have seen
that even on frosty mornings
the humble wattle displays
her summery-yellow sprays

I have noticed
that even through the gloom
of grey cloud's cluster,
the sun pokes his bright toe

I have understood
that, even in the deepest dark,
come splashes of yellow and gold
and descending columns of light.

# Now

Now I remember
how wonderful she was
when she was young and strong
and the lives of all her children
depended on her.

Now I accept
the dark water on which she drifted
as strength of body diminished
and dependency grew.

Now I love her
with more tender understanding,
recognizing how she loved me
in the folly of my youth.

Now I grieve
that something,
I know not what,
stole her best self
and left a smiling shell
carrying a fearful secret
in shuffling co-dependency.

Now I weep
that legacy can be exposed
to bitter entitlement and exploitation.
Who were her advisers?
Should she not have carried
her best self to the ground?
Was she not worthy?
Would that have been too great a sacrifice?

# A Withered Leaf

I wept for her and love her
but I don't grieve for her death.
Death brought release,
freedom from pain and secret guilt.
I grieve that she
grew old and shrunken
and fragile as a withered leaf.

I wept for her and love her
but I don't grieve for material loss,
though no crumbs fell for me
from her ample table.
I grieve that she
grew old and her judgment
shrunk like a withered leaf.

I wept for her and loved her
but I don't grieve for her secrets,
though secrets exclude, and revelation hurts.
I understand her need to pretend.
I grieve that her love,
the guiding light by which she set her course,
became a withered leaf.

# Tapestry

The loom is quiet. Its treadles are still.
The shuttles, once filled with somber weft spools
of darkly shining silk, are almost spent.
Silently I add new shuttles, splice a brighter palate
for an open French door, light, zephyr-lifted curtains,
transparent silver morning light, rich complexity of sun
sparkling on myriad green and the sense of birdsong.
Yes, there must be birdsong. There must be joy.

Yet let me unroll the cloth roller
and look at you for one last time
as you shuffle along your darkened corridor.
It is well before dawn. Those visions of children
which so haunt your sleep have woken you again.
Your stoop is not just the weight of years
but a heavier load of guilt bearing relentlessly down.
Over and over come those terrible words:
"Whatever will people think of me?"

Too late for that now.
I re-roll the cloth.
I have grieved long enough.
Through the open door is blue sky
but I will weave through every scene that remains
those little bits of glowing silk thread that depict
the light of your eyes and the gentleness of your smile.
I must also take one thread of dark somber silk,
a sadly powerful reminder of the tragedy and folly
that comes when independence is surrendered,
when strength of body wanes and the diminished spirit
grows vulnerable and weak.

I re-arrange the shuttles with spools of shining blues,
greens and splashes of gold and vermillion.
I put my foot to the treadle.
With a clatter the parts move,
warp thread absorbs weft
and the tapestry moves on.
Let all your years of goodness outweigh
those final spools of silent, secret surrender.

Now take your peace.
Dream no more.
Wring your hands no more.
Rest quietly.
Sleep easily.
I carry you in my heart
even as I let you go
and with you
all the grief and sorrow
of your last days.
I love you, always,
but now, dear one,
I say goodbye.

Goodbye.
Goodbye.
Goodbye.

*Lear: Be your tears wet? Yes, faith. I pray weep not.*
*If you have poison for me, I will drink it.*
*I know you do not love me; for your sisters*
*Have, as I do remember, done me wrong.*
*You have some cause, they have not.*
*Cordelia: No cause, no cause.*

—*King Lear*, Act IV, Sc 7

# About the Author

Neil Creighton is an Australian poet with a passion for social justice. His work as a teacher has made him aware of the horror of inequality and how opportunity is too often directed by circumstance. Many of his poems reflect his joy in the natural world, especially the creatures and places of his native Australia. Environmental degradation is becoming increasingly important in his poetry. He has been widely published, both in print and online, most often in the USA, but also in Africa, India, and the UK. His chapbook, "Earth Music," will be published by Praxis Magazine Online in 2020 and he is a Contributing Editor for Verse-Virtual, an online poetry journal.

www.ingramcontent.com/pod-product-compliance
Lightning Source LLC
Chambersburg PA
CBHW031154090426
42738CB00008B/1323